# The Power of Personal Branding

## Stand Out and Thrive in Your Career

Harchetan Aneja

Dr Mehak Aneja

The Power of Personal Branding: Stand Out and Thrive in Your Career

Copyright © 2023 by

Harchetan Singh Aneja & Dr Mehak Aneja

Printed by Amazon

ISBN-10: 0645835129

ISBN-13: 9780645835120

First Edition: May 2023

For any queries, feel free to reach out at harchetan@gmail.com

*"Your personal brand is what people say about you when you're not in the room."*

**- Jeff Bezos**
Founder, Executive Chairman, and former
President & CEO of Amazon

# *About the book*

In today's competitive job market, standing out and excelling in your career is essential. "The Power of Personal Branding: Stand Out and Thrive in Your Career" is a comprehensive guide that empowers young professionals to develop a strong personal brand that sets them apart from others and propels their professional growth within organizations.

This book is designed to educate, inspire, and provide practical strategies for building an exceptional personal brand. Drawing on real-life examples and proven techniques, it offers actionable steps to develop essential soft skills, gain recognition from peers, managers, and cross-functional teams, and achieve long-term career success. Readers will learn how to assess their current professional brand, identify their strengths, and craft a compelling personal brand statement that reflects their unique value proposition. They will discover how to build an impressive online presence using social media platforms, particularly leveraging the power of LinkedIn for networking and personal brand promotion.

"The Power of Personal Branding" emphasizes the importance of cultivating professional relationships and provides strategies for effective networking. It also covers developing strong communication skills, showcasing expertise, and positioning oneself as a thought leader in their industry or field. Throughout the book, readers will find practical advice on navigating challenges, overcoming obstacles, and building resilience. They will gain insights into managing their personal brand within their current organization and leveraging opportunities for growth and advancement.

By the end of this book, young professionals will be equipped with the knowledge, tools, and inspiration to cultivate a powerful personal brand that helps them stand out, thrive, and achieve their career aspirations. Whether they are seeking career advancement, looking to make a positive impact, or aiming to secure new opportunities, "The Power of Personal Branding" will be their guide to success.

# About the authors

*Harchetan Singh Aneja*

Harchetan is a seasoned professional with a wealth of experience spanning across automotive, advanced technologies, and medical devices industries. His career has taken him from startups to well-established Fortune 500 companies in Australia, Japan, India, and the USA, providing him with diverse exposure and a deep understanding of industry dynamics. Harchetan brings to the table a unique blend of technical expertise and business acumen, with a focus on Product Management, Development, Lifecycle, and Engineering Management.

Not only is Harchetan an accomplished professional, but he is also a prolific writer and inventor. He has authored technical papers and journal articles published by prestigious organizations such as the Society of Automotive Engineers that were also presented and recognized by industrial experts at the SAE World Congress in the USA. He has a proven track record of successful innovation, with his inventions in the field of medical devices being patented and published. Driven by his passion for innovation and entrepreneurship, Harchetan founded PayMyFees, a startup to revolutionize online fee payments for educational institutes.

In addition, Harchetan feels pride in sharing his knowledge and insights by actively engaging with students and young professionals, providing them with valuable mentorship, guidance, and support in creating impactful resumes and profiles, and as a guest lecturer at various engineering institutes. Harchetan's dedication to helping others navigate their careers has made a significant impact on numerous individuals striving for success.

LinkedIn: https://www.linkedin.com/in/harchetan/

## Dr. Mehak Aneja

Dr. Mehak Aneja is a highly skilled and compassionate medical professional with extensive experience in General Practice, Emergency medicine, and Radiation Oncology. Throughout her career, she has worked at renowned medical institutions in Australia and India, gaining invaluable exposure to diverse cultures, patients from varied social and economic backgrounds, and different healthcare systems and processes. Driven by her deep commitment to providing high-quality medical care, Dr. Aneja continuously seeks opportunities to enhance her knowledge and skills, ensuring that she remains at the forefront of medical advancements to deliver the best possible care to her patients.

Dr. Mehak's experiences as a medical professional bring a unique perspective to this book, particularly considering the challenges and complexities of the healthcare industry. This industry is widely recognized as one of the most demanding and stressful, often leading students and young professionals to face difficult challenges that may cause them to reconsider their career paths or struggle to get deserving recognition. The healthcare sector, with its resource and staff constraints, lack of agility, and limited global collaboration, often struggles to keep pace with the innovative practices seen in leading multinational companies.

By incorporating Dr. Mehak's insights and expertise, this book addresses the specific obstacles and pressures faced by individuals within the healthcare industry. Her firsthand knowledge allows for a comprehensive exploration of the strategies and approaches needed to navigate and thrive in this challenging field. Dr. Mehak's experiences shed light on the importance of resilience, adaptability, and innovation within the healthcare sector.

LinkedIn: https://www.linkedin.com/in/drmehakaneja/

# Table of Contents

# Introduction

Welcome to "The Power of Personal Branding: Stand Out and Thrive in Your Career." In today's fiercely competitive job market, where countless professionals possess similar qualifications and skills, it has become essential to find ways to differentiate yourself and forge a successful career path. That's where the power of personal branding comes into play. Personal branding goes far beyond having a well-designed resume or a polished LinkedIn profile. It involves intentionally crafting and promoting your unique professional identity – a brand that authentically reflects who you are, what you stand for, and the value you bring to the table. It's about cultivating an authentic presence that resonates with others, opens doors to opportunities, and propels your career forward.

The objectives of this book are threefold: to educate, inspire, and provide practical guidance on developing a strong personal brand for exceptional professional and career growth. Within these pages, you will dive into the captivating world of personal branding, learning strategies and techniques to help you stand out from the crowd and thrive in your chosen field.

Chapter 1 sets the foundation by exploring the essence and significance of personal branding. You will discover how a well-crafted personal brand can make a tangible difference in your career trajectory. Real-life examples of individuals who have successfully leveraged personal branding will provide inspiration and insights into the power of this approach.

Chapter 2 guides you through the crucial process of assessing your current brand. Through self-reflection and feedback from trusted sources, you will gain valuable insights into your strengths, weaknesses, and unique attributes. This self-awareness is vital as you begin shaping your personal brand.

Chapter 3 focuses on defining your personal brand. You will clarify your professional goals, identify your target audience, and craft a compelling personal brand statement that authentically represents your value proposition. By aligning your core values and passions with your brand, you will establish a strong foundation for success.

Chapter 4 delves into the realm of building a robust online presence. We will explore strategic techniques for utilizing social media platforms, particularly LinkedIn, to showcase your personal brand and connect with others in your industry. Additionally, we will provide guidance on managing your online reputation and overcoming potential challenges.

In Chapter 5, we shift our focus to cultivating professional relationships. Effective networking strategies, building and nurturing a strong network, and the influential role of mentors and sponsors in advancing your career will be explored.

Chapter 6 takes us into the realm of communication skills, which are an essential component of personal branding. From enhancing verbal and written communication to crafting a captivating elevator pitch, you will gain insights into effectively conveying your personal brand message to others.

Chapter 7 is dedicated to showcasing your expertise. We will guide you in positioning yourself as a thought leader in your field by creating valuable content, participating in industry events, and leveraging professional associations and online communities.

Building a reputation for excellence takes center stage in Chapter 8. We will explore the importance of going above and beyond in your work, cultivating a strong work ethic, pursuing continuous learning, and managing your personal brand within your organization.

Finally, in Chapter 9, we address the challenges and obstacles that may arise on your personal branding journey. From handling criticism to building resilience, you will gain strategies for navigating these hurdles and emerging stronger.

By the end of this book, you will be equipped with the knowledge, tools, and inspiration to cultivate a powerful personal brand that helps you stand out, thrive, and achieve your career aspirations. Whether you are seeking career advancement, looking to make a positive impact, or aiming to secure new opportunities, "The Power of Personal Branding" will serve as your trusted guide on this transformative journey. Let's embark on this exciting exploration of personal branding and discover the limitless potential that lies within you to shape your career and professional life. Happy reading!

# Chapter 1 | Understanding Personal Branding

W elcome to Chapter 1 of "The Power of Personal Branding: Stand Out and Thrive in Your Career." In this chapter, we will delve into the essence and significance of personal branding, providing a deeper understanding of how it can shape your career trajectory and open doors to exciting opportunities. To illustrate the real-world impact of personal branding, we will explore three inspiring examples—one from the technology field, one from finance, and one from marketing. These renowned individuals have leveraged their personal brands to achieve remarkable success and stand out in their respective industries.

## The Power of Personal Branding

Personal branding has become increasingly crucial in today's professional landscape, where competition is fierce and standing out is paramount. It goes beyond traditional qualifications and job titles, encompassing the holistic impression you create as a professional. It is the art of shaping and curating your unique identity, establishing a reputation, and effectively communicating your value proposition to others.

One of the key aspects of personal branding is differentiation. In a crowded marketplace, having a strong personal brand helps you stand out from the competition. It allows you to showcase your unique combination of skills, experiences, and qualities that set you apart. By creating a distinct personal brand, you become memorable and leave a lasting impression on those you encounter.

Another essential aspect of personal branding is credibility. Building a strong personal brand establishes trust and credibility among your peers, colleagues, clients, and employers. It demonstrates your expertise, professionalism, and dedication to your field. When your personal brand exudes credibility, it becomes easier to attract opportunities, gain the trust of others, and build meaningful relationships.

Furthermore, personal branding facilitates effective networking and relationship building. When you have a clear personal brand, it becomes easier for others to understand what you bring to the table. This clarity allows you to connect with like-minded individuals, mentors, and potential collaborators who align with your personal brand and share your values and aspirations. By leveraging your personal brand, you can foster valuable professional relationships that can propel your career forward.

A well-crafted personal brand also allows you to navigate career transitions and seize new opportunities. As you evolve and explore different paths in your professional journey, your personal brand becomes a cohesive thread that ties your experiences together. It serves as a compass, guiding you towards opportunities that align with your brand and contribute to your long-term goals.

Ultimately, personal branding is about owning your narrative and shaping how others perceive you. It is about intentional self-presentation and managing the impressions you make. By proactively managing your personal brand, you have the power to influence how others perceive your expertise, credibility, and potential. When done effectively, personal branding can open doors to exciting opportunities, attract collaborations, and position you as a sought-after professional in your industry.

By understanding and harnessing the power of personal branding, you can shape your professional identity, build credibility, and stand out in today's competitive job market. In the following chapters, we will explore practical strategies and actionable steps to help you develop and strengthen your personal brand, unlocking the full potential of your career aspirations.

## Real-life Examples
To further illustrate the impact of personal branding, let's explore three real-life examples from different industries.

## Technology
Elon Musk, the visionary entrepreneur and CEO of Tesla, SpaceX, and Neuralink, has established a personal brand that is synonymous with innovation, ambition, and pushing

the boundaries of what is possible. Through his remarkable achievements and charismatic leadership style, Musk has become one of the most influential figures in the technology and space exploration industries.

One of the key elements of Musk's personal brand is his unwavering commitment to pursuing ambitious goals. From the early days of SpaceX, when many doubted the feasibility of private space exploration, Musk set out to revolutionize the aerospace industry. His bold vision of establishing a colony on Mars and making humanity a multi-planetary species has captured the imagination of people worldwide. Through his relentless pursuit of these audacious goals, Musk has positioned himself as a pioneer and a true visionary.

Another aspect of Musk's personal brand is his ability to leverage the power of storytelling. He excels at articulating his vision in a compelling manner, inspiring not only his employees and stakeholders but also the general public. Musk effectively communicates the potential impact of his ventures on society and emphasizes the importance of sustainable energy and exploration of space.

Musk's personal brand also benefits from his active presence on social media platforms, particularly Twitter. His candid and often unconventional tweets have gained widespread attention and have become a trademark of his online persona. Musk uses social media as a platform to share updates on his companies, engage with his followers, and even address criticism. This direct and unfiltered communication style has allowed him to connect with a broad audience and cultivate a dedicated following.

Furthermore, Musk's personal brand is strengthened by his reputation as a risk-taker and a disruptor. He is known for challenging established norms and traditional ways of doing things. Whether it's revolutionizing the automotive industry with Tesla's electric vehicles or revolutionizing space travel with SpaceX's reusable rockets, Musk consistently pushes the boundaries and inspires others to think differently.

Finance

Warren Buffett, the legendary investor and CEO of Berkshire Hathaway, has built a personal brand that is synonymous with value investing, wisdom, and long-term success. His journey to becoming one of the wealthiest individuals in the world is a testament to his disciplined approach and exceptional business acumen.

One of the key factors in Buffett's personal brand is his investment philosophy centered around value investing. He is renowned for his ability to identify undervalued companies with strong fundamentals and long-term growth potential. Buffett's disciplined approach to investing, focusing on intrinsic value rather than short-term market fluctuations, has earned him the reputation of being a patient and astute investor.

Another aspect of Buffett's personal brand is his emphasis on simplicity and transparency. He is known for his straightforward communication style, avoiding complex financial jargon and presenting his investment insights in a relatable manner. Buffett's annual shareholder letters and interviews are eagerly anticipated by investors and aspiring entrepreneurs alike, as they offer valuable insights into his investment strategies and overall business philosophy.

Furthermore, Buffett's personal brand is built on his reputation for integrity and ethical business practices. He has consistently emphasized the importance of conducting business with honesty, transparency, and a long-term perspective. Buffett's commitment to ethical behavior and his philanthropic efforts, such as the Giving Pledge, have further enhanced his reputation as a trusted and respected figure in the business world.

Buffett's personal brand is also influenced by his frugal lifestyle and humble demeanor. Despite his immense wealth, he has maintained a modest lifestyle, living in the same house he bought decades ago and often opting for simple pleasures. This down-to-earth approach has resonated with many, contributing to his image as a wise and relatable investor.

Marketing

Gary Vaynerchuk, a serial entrepreneur, author, and motivational speaker, has built a personal brand that is synonymous with hustle, authenticity, and entrepreneurial success. Through his relentless work ethic and unique approach to content creation, Vaynerchuk has become a prominent figure in the world of business and personal development.

One of the cornerstones of Vaynerchuk's personal brand is his emphasis on hustle and hard work. He believes in putting in the hours, consistently grinding, and seizing opportunities to achieve success. Vaynerchuk's own journey from running a wine business to building a multi-million dollar media empire serves as a testament to the power of hard work and determination.

Another key aspect of Vaynerchuk's personal brand is his authenticity and unfiltered communication style. He is known for his no-nonsense, tell-it-like-it-is approach, which resonates with his audience. Vaynerchuk uses various platforms, including social media, podcasts, and public speaking engagements, to share his experiences, insights, and advice on entrepreneurship and personal development. By being transparent about both his successes and failures, Vaynerchuk has garnered a loyal following who appreciate his genuine and relatable approach.

Furthermore, Vaynerchuk's personal brand is rooted in his expertise in digital marketing and social media. He was an early adopter of platforms like YouTube, Twitter, and Instagram, leveraging them to grow his personal brand and reach a wider audience. Vaynerchuk's insights on social media marketing and building an online presence have positioned him as a thought leader in the industry.

Vaynerchuk's personal brand is also characterized by his boundless energy and enthusiasm. He exudes passion in his content and engagements, inspiring others to pursue their passions and embrace entrepreneurship. Vaynerchuk's motivational speeches and books, such as "Crushing It!" and "Jab, Jab, Jab, Right Hook," have become go-to resources for individuals seeking guidance and inspiration in their entrepreneurial journeys.

## Insights from Real-Life Examples

These real-life examples of Elon Musk, Warren Buffett, and Gary Vaynerchuk provide profound insights into the world of personal branding.

Firstly, they all embraced their authentic selves and showcased their unique perspectives. They understood that their personal brands should reflect their values, passions, and expertise.

Secondly, they consistently created and shared valuable content. Whether it was Musk's visionary speeches,

Buffett's insightful letters, or Vaynerchuk's engaging videos, they actively contributed to their industries and built credibility through their knowledge sharing.

Thirdly, they cultivated a strong online and offline presence. They leveraged platforms like social media, conferences, and public speaking engagements to connect with their audiences, engage in conversations, and build communities around their personal brands.

Lastly, they each had a clear and compelling narrative. Musk's ambition to transform transportation and space exploration, Buffett's value investing principles, and Vaynerchuk's passion for entrepreneurship and hustle became central themes in their personal brands.

## Conclusion

Chapter 1 has provided a deeper understanding of personal branding and its significance in shaping a successful career. Through the illustrious examples of Elon Musk, Warren Buffett, and Gary Vaynerchuk, we have witnessed how personal branding can propel individuals to become influential leaders in their respective fields. By embracing authenticity, sharing valuable content, cultivating a strong presence, and crafting a compelling narrative, these renowned individuals have harnessed the power of personal branding to leave a lasting impact on their industries. As we continue our exploration, you will gain actionable strategies and techniques to develop and enhance your own personal brand, unlocking the full potential of your career journey.

# Chapter 2 | Assessing Your Current Brand

In Chapter 2, we embark on a transformative journey of self-reflection and assessment, aiming to gain a deeper understanding of your current personal brand. This process is vital as it lays the foundation for shaping and enhancing one's personal brand in alignment with your career goals. By objectively evaluating your strengths, weaknesses, and unique attributes, you will gain valuable insights that will guide your personal branding efforts and set you on a path towards success.

## Reflecting on Your Professional Journey

In this section, take the time to reflect on your professional journey thus far. Consider your career accomplishments, experiences, and milestones. Reflect on the projects you have successfully completed, the skills you have acquired, and the impact you have made in your field. Reflecting on your journey allows you to acknowledge your progress, strengths, and areas of expertise. It provides a holistic view of your professional growth and helps you identify key themes and strengths that form the basis of your personal brand.

### Self-Activity

Create a timeline of your professional journey, noting down significant accomplishments, projects, and skills acquired along the way. Reflect on the challenges you have overcome and the achievements you are proud of. This exercise will help you recognize your unique contributions and strengths.

## Gathering Feedback from Others

Seeking feedback from trusted sources is invaluable in understanding how your personal brand is perceived by others. Reach out to colleagues, mentors, managers, and clients who have worked closely with you and request their honest input. Ask for their perspectives on your strengths, areas for improvement, and the unique qualities they associate with you. This external feedback provides valuable insights into how others perceive your personal brand, helping you identify any gaps or opportunities for growth.

### Self-Activity

Create a feedback questionnaire to gather input from those you trust. Ask open-ended questions such as "What do you believe are my key strengths?", "How would you describe my professional style?", and "What unique qualities do you think I bring to the table?". Analyze the feedback received to identify recurring themes and gain a comprehensive understanding of how your personal brand is perceived.

## Identifying Your Unique Attributes

Building upon your reflections and feedback, it's time to identify and articulate your unique attributes that differentiate you from others in your industry. Consider your core values, passions, skills, and strengths. Reflect on what makes you stand out and what sets you apart. Think about the qualities that are highly valued in your field and how you embody them. By identifying these unique attributes, you can start shaping your personal brand around them, aligning your professional identity with your authentic self.

### Self-Activity

Make a list of your core values, passions, and strengths. Reflect on how these attributes manifest in your professional life and how they contribute to your personal brand. Consider how you can leverage these attributes to create a compelling and authentic personal brand that resonates with your target audience.

## Assessing Your Online Presence

In today's digital age, your online presence plays a significant role in shaping your personal brand. Conduct a comprehensive audit of your online profiles, such as

LinkedIn, professional websites, and social media accounts. Evaluate the consistency, professionalism, and alignment of your online presence with your desired personal brand. Ensure that your online presence reflects your expertise, values, and the image you want to portray to your target audience.

Self-Activity

Review your online profiles and content. Consider the following questions: Is the information up-to-date and accurate? Does your online presence reflect your professional brand? Are the visuals, language, and tone consistent with your desired personal brand? Make necessary updates and adjustments to align your online presence with your personal brand and career goals.

## Identifying Areas for Improvement

As you assess your personal brand, it is essential to identify areas for improvement. Be open to acknowledging any weaknesses or gaps in your current brand. This self-awareness allows you to address these areas proactively and develop strategies for growth. Consider investing in professional development, training, or seeking mentorship to enhance the aspects of your personal brand that require refinement.

**Self-Activity**

Identify two areas for improvement in your personal brand. Research professional development opportunities or resources that can help you grow in these areas. Set specific goals and develop an action plan to bridge the gaps and enhance your personal brand.

## Creating Your Personal Brand Statement

A personal brand statement succinctly captures the essence of your personal brand. It is a concise, compelling statement that communicates who you are, what you do, and the value you offer. Based on your reflections, feedback, and unique attributes, craft a personal brand statement that resonates with your target audience and reflects your career aspirations. Your personal brand statement will serve as a guiding light throughout your personal branding journey.

**Self-Activity**

Develop your personal brand statement by summarizing your unique attributes, strengths, and the value you bring to your profession. Craft a concise and impactful statement that accurately represents your personal brand and the impact you aspire to make in your field. Refine and iterate on your personal brand statement until it accurately captures your essence.

## Conclusion

Chapter 2 has provided guidance on assessing your personal brand. By reflecting on your professional journey, gathering feedback, identifying your unique attributes, assessing your online presence, and identifying areas for improvement, you have gained valuable insights into your current personal brand. This self-assessment sets the stage for shaping your personal brand in alignment with your career goals. In the upcoming chapters, we will delve deeper into strategies and techniques to refine and amplify your personal brand, empowering you to stand out and thrive in your chosen field.

# Chapter 3 | Crafting Your Personal Brand Strategy

In this chapter, we will delve into the exciting process of crafting your personal brand strategy. Armed with a deeper understanding of your current personal brand, it's time to shape and refine your brand to align with your career aspirations. By developing a clear and intentional personal brand strategy, you will create a roadmap for success and establish yourself as a standout professional in your field.

## Defining Your Target Audience

To create a compelling personal brand, it's crucial to identify and understand your target audience. Consider the individuals or groups who can benefit from your expertise, skills, and unique attributes. Define their characteristics, needs, and preferences. By understanding your target audience, you can tailor your personal brand to resonate with them, effectively positioning yourself as the solution to their challenges or aspirations.

### Example

If you are a marketing professional specializing in digital marketing for startups, your target audience may consist of early-stage entrepreneurs or small business owners who are seeking guidance on establishing a strong online presence and driving customer acquisition. Understanding their pain points, goals, and the specific challenges they face will help you tailor your personal brand messaging and content to address their needs effectively.

## Defining Your Unique Value Proposition

Your unique value proposition (UVP) encapsulates the distinctive value you offer to your target audience. It highlights what sets you apart and why others should choose you over competitors. Define the unique combination of skills, experiences, and qualities that make you stand out. Your UVP should address the specific needs, desires, or challenges of your target audience and articulate how you can fulfill them uniquely.

### Example

Suppose you are a software engineer specializing in artificial intelligence and machine learning. Your unique value proposition could be that you possess a deep understanding of both the technical aspects and the practical applications of AI/ML. You can communicate that you are not only skilled in developing cutting-edge algorithms but also proficient in translating complex concepts into business solutions. This UVP distinguishes you from other software engineers who may have expertise in either technical aspects or business applications, but not both.

## Developing Your Brand Identity

Your brand identity encompasses the visual and verbal elements that communicate your personal brand to the world. It includes your brand name, logo, colors, typography, and overall visual aesthetic. Additionally, it encompasses your tone of voice, language, and communication style. Developing a cohesive and consistent brand identity is essential for building recognition and conveying professionalism.

### Example

Let's say you are a freelance graphic designer known for your vibrant and bold design style. Your brand identity could reflect these qualities by using a vibrant color palette, bold typography, and a dynamic logo that represents your creative approach. Additionally, your tone of voice in your brand communications could be energetic, engaging, and conversational, reflecting your approachable and collaborative nature.

## Building Your Online Presence

In today's digital era, building a strong online presence is crucial for personal branding. Establish a compelling and professional online presence that showcases your expertise, personality, and achievements. Leverage platforms such as LinkedIn, personal websites, and social media channels to share your insights, engage with your target audience, and build a network of professional connections.

## Example

Suppose you are a finance professional aiming to establish yourself as a thought leader in the field. You can build your online presence by regularly sharing insightful articles, analyses, and commentary on finance-related topics through your LinkedIn profile. You can create a professional website that showcases your expertise, displays your achievements and certifications, and offers a platform for potential clients or employers to contact you. Additionally, you can actively engage with your target audience by participating in relevant industry groups, commenting on relevant posts, and sharing valuable resources.

## Cultivating Your Professional Network

Building a strong professional network is essential for personal branding and career growth. Actively seek opportunities to connect with like-minded professionals, mentors, influencers, and industry leaders. Engage in networking events, join professional organizations, and participate in online communities to expand your network. Nurture these relationships by offering support, sharing insights, and collaborating on projects.

## Example

Imagine you are a healthcare professional specializing in public health. To cultivate your professional network, you can attend conferences and workshops related to public health, where you can meet experts in the field and engage in meaningful conversations. You can also join professional organizations such as the American Public Health Association (APHA) or local public health associations, which provide networking opportunities and access to valuable resources. Additionally, you can participate in online communities, forums, or social media groups dedicated to public health, where you can share your knowledge, connect with peers, and establish your credibility in the field.

## Conclusion

Chapter 3 has guided you through the process of crafting your personal brand strategy. By defining your target audience, identifying your unique value proposition, developing your brand identity, building your online presence, and cultivating your professional network, you are laying a solid foundation for an impactful personal brand. In the upcoming chapters, we will explore strategies to amplify your personal brand and effectively communicate your value proposition to attract new opportunities and excel in your career.

# Chapter 4 | Building an Engaging Online Presence

Here, we explore the importance of building an engaging online presence for personal branding. In today's digital landscape, establishing a strong online presence is essential for reaching a wider audience, showcasing your expertise, and building credibility. This chapter will provide you with practical strategies and techniques to effectively leverage various online platforms to enhance your personal brand and engage with your target audience.

## Optimizing Your LinkedIn Profile

LinkedIn is a powerful platform for professionals to connect, network, and showcase their skills and experiences. In this section, we will discuss key elements of an optimized LinkedIn profile and provide tips to make your profile stand out.

- Profile Picture and Headline: Choose a professional and high-quality profile picture that represents your personal brand. Craft a compelling headline that highlights your expertise, key skills, or unique value proposition. Make sure it grabs attention and clearly communicates your professional identity.

- Summary Section: Craft a well-written and concise summary that encapsulates your professional background, key achievements, and career aspirations. Use this section to showcase your unique selling points, career goals, and the value you bring to employers or clients. Incorporate relevant keywords to increase the visibility of your profile in search results.

- Experience and Accomplishments: Provide detailed information about your professional experience, including job titles, companies, and a description of your roles and responsibilities. Highlight significant accomplishments, projects, or results you have achieved. Use bullet points to make the information easily scannable and showcase the value you delivered in each role.

- Skills and Endorsements: List your key skills and areas of expertise. Be selective and focus on skills that align with your personal brand and professional goals. Request endorsements from colleagues, supervisors, or clients who can vouch for your skills and abilities. Endorse others in return to build a reciprocal network of credibility.

- Recommendations: Seek recommendations from colleagues, clients, or mentors who can provide testimonials about your work ethic, expertise, or character. These recommendations add credibility and strengthen your personal brand. Reach out to individuals you have worked closely with and kindly request their support in writing a recommendation.

- Engage in Groups and Content Sharing: Join industry-related groups and actively engage in discussions. Share relevant articles, insights, or thought-provoking content to establish yourself as a knowledgeable professional. Engaging with others' posts, leaving thoughtful comments, and sharing valuable resources demonstrate your expertise and expand your network.

- Regular Updates: Regularly update your profile with new achievements, projects, or skills. Share updates about your professional milestones, certifications, or relevant industry news. Stay active on LinkedIn by posting content, engaging with others, and nurturing your professional relationships.

Optimizing your LinkedIn profile allows you to present yourself effectively to potential employers, clients, or collaborators. By showcasing your expertise, accomplishments, and thought leadership, you enhance your personal brand, increase your visibility, and attract meaningful connections and opportunities.

## Creating Valuable Content

Creating valuable content is a powerful way to establish yourself as an authority in your industry and build a strong personal brand. By sharing insightful and relevant content, you can attract and engage your target audience, demonstrate your expertise, and provide value to others. Here are some key strategies for creating valuable content:

- Understand Your Audience: Gain a deep understanding of your target audience—their needs, pain points, and interests. This knowledge will guide you in creating content that resonates with them and provides solutions or valuable insights.

- Choose the Right Format: Consider the most effective format for delivering your content. It could be blog posts, articles, videos, podcasts, infographics, or webinars. Select formats that align with your strengths, expertise, and the preferences of your audience.

- Share Actionable Insights: Create content that offers practical advice, tips, or step-by-step guides. Your audience should be able to apply the insights you provide to improve their skills, solve problems, or achieve their goals.

- Stay Current and Relevant: Stay up-to-date with the latest trends, research, and developments in your industry. Share timely and relevant content that addresses emerging topics or challenges, demonstrating your knowledge and expertise in real-time.

- Engage with Your Audience: Encourage interaction and engagement with your content. Respond to comments, questions, and feedback from your audience. This fosters a sense of community, builds trust, and encourages further conversation.

- Collaborate with Others: Collaborate with industry peers, influencers, or subject matter experts to create joint content. This not only provides different perspectives but also expands your reach to their audience, introducing you to new followers and potential connections.

- Repurpose and Amplify: Repurpose your content across multiple channels to maximize its reach. For example, turn a blog post into a podcast episode or create an infographic summarizing key points. Share your content on social media platforms, industry forums, or relevant online communities to amplify its visibility.

By consistently creating valuable content, you position yourself as a go-to resource in your field. Your content establishes your expertise, builds credibility, and strengthens your personal brand. Providing value to your audience through your content establishes a meaningful connection and opens doors to new opportunities and collaborations.

## Example

Suppose you are a software engineer with expertise in mobile app development. You can create valuable content by writing articles or creating video tutorials that explain best practices, tips, and techniques in mobile app development. You can cover topics like optimizing app performance, implementing user-friendly interfaces, or integrating new technologies. By sharing your knowledge and insights, you position yourself as a go-to resource for developers and gain visibility within your industry.

## Engaging on Social Media

Social media platforms provide a powerful avenue to engage with your target audience, establish your personal brand, and expand your professional network. Engaging effectively on social media can help you build credibility, attract opportunities, and stay connected with industry trends. Here are key strategies for engaging on social media:

- Select the Right Platforms: Identify the social media platforms that are most relevant to your industry and target audience. LinkedIn, Twitter, and

Instagram are popular choices for professional networking and industry engagement. Choose platforms where your target audience is active and where you can showcase your expertise effectively.

- Share Relevant Content: Consistently share valuable and relevant content that aligns with your personal brand and interests your audience. This can include industry news, thought leadership articles, blog posts, or curated content that provides insights or sparks conversations. Use a mix of text, images, and videos to make your content visually appealing and engaging.

- Participate in Discussions: Engage in industry-related discussions, groups, or forums on social media platforms. Contribute thoughtful comments, share your insights, and ask relevant questions. Actively participating in discussions helps you build connections, establish your expertise, and stay on top of industry trends.

- Connect and Collaborate: Use social media platforms to connect with professionals, industry influencers, and like-minded individuals. Engage with their content by liking, commenting, and sharing. Cultivate meaningful connections and collaborations that can lead to opportunities, partnerships, or mentorship.

- Personalize Your Interactions: When engaging with others on social media, personalize your interactions. Address individuals by their names, acknowledge their contributions, and provide thoughtful responses. Show genuine interest in their work and establish rapport by asking relevant questions or sharing relevant resources.

- Maintain Professionalism: While social media allows for more casual interactions, it's important to maintain professionalism and integrity. Be mindful of your tone, language, and the content you share. Avoid engaging in controversial or divisive discussions that may harm your personal brand.

- Analyze and Adapt: Regularly review the performance of your social media efforts. Analyze engagement metrics, such as likes, comments, shares, and follower growth. Use these insights to refine your content strategy, understand what resonates with your audience, and make adjustments as needed.

By actively engaging on social media, you can enhance your personal brand, expand your network, and stay connected with industry trends and conversations. Consistent engagement builds your reputation, establishes you as a trusted professional, and positions you for valuable opportunities within your field.

## Example

Suppose you are a fitness trainer targeting a younger demographic. Platforms like Instagram or TikTok may be more suitable for engaging with your audience. You can create visually appealing content showcasing workout routines, healthy recipes, and motivational messages. Engage with your followers by responding to comments, asking questions, and encouraging them to share their fitness goals. Collaborate with fitness influencers by conducting joint workouts or featuring each other's content, which can help expand your reach to a wider audience.

## Conclusion

Chapter 4 has provided you with valuable insights and strategies for building an engaging online presence. By optimizing your LinkedIn profile, creating valuable content, and engaging on social media, you can establish a strong and influential personal brand. In the next chapter, we will explore techniques to network effectively and leverage your personal brand to unlock new opportunities and advance in your career.

# Chapter 5 | Cultivating Professional Relationships

L et's explore the art of cultivating professional relationships and building a strong network. Cultivating meaningful connections is essential for career growth, as it opens doors to new opportunities, provides support and guidance, and expands your knowledge and perspectives. This chapter will provide you with strategies and techniques to build and nurture a strong professional network, effective networking techniques, the importance of developing meaningful connections, and the role of mentors and sponsors in your professional journey.

## Strategies for Building and Nurturing a Strong Network

Building a strong professional network is essential for career growth and personal branding. A robust network can open doors to new opportunities, provide valuable insights, and support your professional development. Here are key strategies for building and nurturing a strong network:

- Define Your Networking Goals: Clarify your networking objectives to ensure you have a clear direction. Identify the types of professionals you want to connect with, the industries or fields you're interested in, and the specific outcomes you hope to achieve through networking. This clarity will guide your networking efforts.

- Attend Industry Events: Actively participate in industry events, conferences, seminars, and workshops relevant to your field. These gatherings provide excellent opportunities to meet professionals, exchange ideas, and build connections. Prepare a brief introduction and engaging conversation starters to make a memorable impression.

- Leverage Online Networking Platforms: Utilize online platforms such as LinkedIn, professional forums, and industry-specific communities to expand your network. Actively engage in discussions, share valuable insights, and connect with professionals who align with your interests and goals. Seek opportunities to collaborate or contribute to industry conversations.

- Seek Informational Interviews: Request informational interviews with professionals you admire or who work in your target industry. These interviews provide an opportunity to learn from their experiences, gain valuable insights, and potentially establish mentorship relationships. Prepare thoughtful questions and demonstrate a genuine interest in their expertise.

- Offer Help and Support: Networking is a two-way street. Be proactive in offering help and support to your network. Share valuable resources, make introductions, or offer your expertise where applicable. Providing value to others strengthens your relationships and fosters a reciprocal environment of support.

- Attend Networking Events and Meetups: Attend local networking events, meetups, or industry-specific gatherings to connect with professionals in your area. These events provide a more casual setting for building relationships and exchanging ideas. Be approachable, listen actively, and follow up with individuals you meet to nurture the connection.

- Maintain Regular Communication: Networking is not a one-time activity but an ongoing process. Stay in touch with your connections by regularly reaching out, sending relevant articles or resources, and checking in on their professional endeavors. Building and nurturing relationships requires consistent effort and genuine interest in others' success.

By implementing these strategies, you can build a strong and diverse professional network. Remember, networking is not just about collecting contacts but about building meaningful connections based on mutual support and shared interests. A robust network can provide invaluable support throughout your career and contribute to your overall professional growth.

## Example

Suppose you are a marketing professional looking to build a strong network in the digital marketing industry. You can start by attending marketing conferences, joining relevant LinkedIn groups, and participating in online forums where you can connect with professionals in your field. Actively engage in conversations, share insights, and offer support. Follow up with new connections by sending personalized messages and finding ways to add value to their professional journey.

## Effective Networking Techniques

Networking is not just about meeting new people, but also about building meaningful connections and nurturing relationships. To make your networking efforts more effective, consider the following techniques:

- Be Authentic and Genuine: Approach networking with an authentic and genuine mindset. Be yourself and show a sincere interest in getting to know others. People appreciate authenticity and are more likely to engage in meaningful conversations with someone who is genuine.

- Active Listening: Practice active listening when engaging with others. Pay attention to what they are saying, ask follow-up questions, and show genuine interest in their experiences and perspectives. Active listening not only helps you build rapport but also allows you to understand others' needs and find ways to offer support.

- Provide Value: Seek ways to provide value to others in your network. Share relevant resources, offer your expertise or assistance, and make connections that can benefit both parties. By providing value, you establish yourself as a valuable and trusted contact within your network.

- Follow Up and Follow Through: After meeting someone, always follow up to express your appreciation for the conversation and any promises made. This shows professionalism and reinforces the connection. Follow through on any commitments or offers of help that you made during the conversation.

- Cultivate Relationships: Networking is not just about making connections; it's about cultivating relationships over time. Maintain regular contact with your network by reaching out, offering support, and staying updated on their professional endeavors. Cultivating relationships helps you build a strong network that can support your career growth.

- Seek Mutual Benefits: Networking is a mutually beneficial process. Look for ways to help others while also seeking support and opportunities for yourself. When networking, focus on creating win-win situations where both parties can gain value from the relationship.

- Practice Effective Communication: Develop effective communication skills, both verbal and written. Be clear, concise, and articulate when expressing yourself. Pay attention to your body language, tone, and non-verbal cues during in-person networking events.

Example

Imagine you are attending a networking event for entrepreneurs. Instead of simply talking about yourself and your accomplishments, actively listen to others and show genuine interest in their ventures. Ask questions that go beyond small talk and delve into their challenges, goals, and successes. By demonstrating a genuine desire to learn from and support others, you foster meaningful connections that can lead to future collaborations or business opportunities.

## Developing Meaningful Connections

Meaningful connections are built on trust, shared values, and common interests. Developing meaningful connections goes beyond surface-level networking and involves building deeper relationships based on shared values, trust, and genuine connections. Here are some key points to consider:

- Shared Interests and Values: Look for individuals who share similar interests, values, or professional goals. Commonalities form the foundation of strong connections and provide a solid basis for meaningful relationships.

- Authenticity and Vulnerability: Be open and authentic in your interactions. Share your aspirations, challenges, and experiences. By being vulnerable, you create a space for others to open up as well, leading to more meaningful and supportive connections.

- Active Engagement: Actively engage with individuals in your network. Attend industry events, participate in discussions, and join professional groups or associations. Show genuine interest in others' work, ask insightful questions, and provide meaningful contributions to foster deeper connections.

- Empathy and Support: Practice empathy and offer support to your connections. Show understanding, listen attentively, and provide guidance or resources when needed. Be a source of encouragement and motivation for others, and they will be more likely to reciprocate.

- Foster Trust and Reliability: Build trust by being reliable and following through on your commitments. Be someone others can count on, whether it's offering assistance, providing introductions, or delivering on promises. Trust is a fundamental element of meaningful connections.

- Maintain Regular Communication: Stay in touch with your connections by regularly reaching out and checking in on their progress. Schedule catch-up meetings, send thoughtful messages, and share relevant opportunities or resources. Consistent communication helps maintain and strengthen the connection over time.

- Collaborate and Share: Seek opportunities to collaborate with individuals in your network. By working together on projects, sharing knowledge, or supporting each other's initiatives, you deepen the bond and create meaningful connections based on mutual growth.

Remember, developing meaningful connections is a long-term investment that requires time, effort, and genuine interest. By nurturing these connections, you create a supportive network that can provide guidance, opportunities, and emotional support throughout your professional journey.

## Mentors and Sponsors

Mentors and sponsors play a crucial role in career advancement by offering guidance, support, and opportunities, thus, playing a crucial role in personal and professional development. They provide guidance, support, and opportunities for growth. Here are some key points to consider regarding mentors and sponsors:

- Mentors: Mentors are experienced professionals who offer guidance, advice, and wisdom based on their own expertise and experiences. They provide valuable insights, help navigate challenges, and offer a fresh perspective on career development. A mentor can be someone within your organization, industry, or a trusted professional outside your immediate network.

- Finding a Mentor: Seek mentors who align with your career goals and aspirations. Look for individuals who possess the skills, knowledge, and experience you want to develop. Approach potential mentors with a clear understanding of what you hope to gain from the relationship and express your genuine interest in their guidance.

- Building a Mentoring Relationship: Establish an open and honest relationship with your mentor. Be proactive in seeking their advice and feedback, and show appreciation for their time and expertise. Actively listen to their insights, ask thoughtful questions, and apply their guidance to your professional growth.

- Sponsors: Sponsors are influential individuals who advocate for your career advancement and provide opportunities for growth. They use their position and influence to endorse you, recommend you for projects, promotions, or new roles, and actively support your professional development.

- Developing Sponsorship Relationships: Cultivate relationships with sponsors by demonstrating your skills, expertise, and potential. Build a reputation for excellence in your work, take on challenging projects, and seek visibility within your organization or industry. Develop meaningful connections with influential individuals who can become sponsors and support your career progression.

- Reciprocity: Both mentorship and sponsorship relationships require reciprocity. Show gratitude for the guidance and opportunities provided by mentors and sponsors. Offer your assistance, share your knowledge, and be willing to support their endeavors. Building a mutually beneficial relationship strengthens the bond and ensures a long-lasting connection.

- Continuous Growth and Evolution: As you progress in your career, your mentorship and sponsorship needs may change. Be open to evolving relationships and seek new mentors or sponsors who can provide guidance and opportunities at different stages of your professional journey.

By cultivating relationships with mentors and sponsors, you gain access to invaluable guidance, support, and opportunities that can accelerate your career growth. Actively seek out mentors, develop meaningful connections, and nurture these relationships to enhance your personal and professional development.

Example

Let's say you are an aspiring engineer seeking a mentor in the aerospace industry. Look for experienced professionals who have achieved success in your desired field. Reach out to them with a genuine request for mentorship, expressing your admiration for their work and your eagerness to learn from their experiences. Nurture this mentorship relationship by scheduling regular meetings or check-ins, seeking their guidance on career decisions, and incorporating their advice into your professional development.

## Conclusion

Chapter 5 has provided you with valuable insights into cultivating professional relationships and building a strong network. By employing effective networking strategies, developing meaningful connections, and seeking mentors and sponsors, you enhance your career prospects and open doors to new opportunities. In the next chapter, we will explore the power of personal branding in networking and how to leverage your unique qualities to make a lasting impression.

# Chapter 6 | Developing Effective Communication Skills

This chapter uncovers the critical role of effective communication skills in personal branding and career success. Communication is a powerful tool that allows you to convey your ideas, influence others, and establish strong connections. This chapter will provide you with strategies to enhance both verbal and written communication, craft compelling elevator pitches and professional bios, master public speaking and presentations, and utilize storytelling to convey your personal brand. Engaging in self-activities throughout the chapter will help you practice and apply these skills in real-world scenarios.

## Enhancing Verbal and Written Communication

Verbal and written communication are fundamental skills for professional success. In this section, we delve into strategies for enhancing both verbal and written communication to strengthen your personal brand and make a lasting impression:

### Verbal Communication

Mastering verbal communication involves articulating your thoughts clearly, confidently, and persuasively. It is essential for presentations, meetings, networking events, and everyday interactions. Here are key strategies to enhance your verbal communication skills:

1.  Clarity and Conciseness: Practice expressing your ideas in a clear and concise manner. Use simple language, avoid jargon, and organize your thoughts effectively to ensure your message is easily understood.

2.  Active Listening: Develop active listening skills to engage in meaningful conversations. Listen attentively, ask clarifying questions, and show genuine interest in others' perspectives. Effective communication involves not just speaking but also being receptive to others.

3.  Non-Verbal Communication: Pay attention to your non-verbal cues, such as body language, facial expressions, and tone of voice. Project confidence, maintain eye contact, and use appropriate gestures to convey your message effectively.

Written Communication
Strong written communication skills are essential for crafting compelling emails, reports, social media posts, and other written content. Here are strategies to enhance your written communication skills:

1. Clarity and Structure: Write in a clear and organized manner, ensuring your message is easily comprehensible. Use concise sentences, logical paragraphs, and headings/subheadings to improve readability.

2. Grammar and Spelling: Pay attention to grammar, punctuation, and spelling to ensure your written content is error-free and professional. Proofread your work carefully or use proofreading tools to catch any mistakes.

3. Tailoring Your Message: Adapt your writing style and tone to suit the intended audience and purpose. Whether it's a formal business email or a social media post, tailor your message to resonate with the reader.

Remember, enhancing verbal and written communication skills requires practice and feedback. Seek opportunities to engage in public speaking, join Toastmasters or other speaking clubs, and actively write and seek feedback on your written content. By continuously improving your communication skills, you will not only strengthen your personal brand but also build strong connections, influence others, and convey your expertise effectively.

## Self-activity
Choose a topic of interest and deliver a short presentation to a small group of colleagues or friends. Focus on

incorporating the techniques learned to enhance your verbal communication skills. Afterward, solicit feedback from the audience on your clarity, delivery, and overall impact.

## Crafting an Elevator Pitch and Professional Bios

Crafting a compelling elevator pitch and professional bios is crucial for effectively communicating your personal brand and making a memorable impression. In this section, we explore strategies for creating concise and impactful introductions that capture the essence of your personal brand:

### Elevator Pitch

An elevator pitch is a concise and persuasive summary of who you are, what you do, and the value you bring. It is called an elevator pitch because it should be brief enough to deliver in the time it takes to ride an elevator. Here are key strategies for crafting an elevator pitch:

- Know Your Audience: Tailor your elevator pitch to the specific audience you are addressing. Understand their needs, challenges, and interests, and highlight how your skills and expertise can address those.

- Focus on Unique Value Proposition: Clearly articulate the unique value you bring and what sets you apart from others in your field. Highlight your strengths, accomplishments, and the specific benefits you offer.

- Practice and Refine: Craft a concise and engaging pitch and practice it until it flows naturally. Seek feedback from trusted peers or mentors and refine your pitch based on their suggestions.

## Professional Bios

Professional bios provide a snapshot of your professional background, achievements, and expertise. They are often used on websites, social media profiles, or professional networking platforms. Here are strategies for creating impactful professional bios:

- Highlight Relevant Achievements: Summarize your key accomplishments, experiences, and qualifications that are most relevant to your personal brand and target audience. Focus on showcasing your expertise and credibility.

- Use Compelling Language: Write in a tone that reflects your personal brand and captures attention. Use powerful and concise language to convey your achievements and values.

- Tailor for Different Platforms: Adapt your professional bio for different platforms, considering the specific requirements and character limits of each. Customize your bio to align with the platform's audience and purpose.

Crafting an elevator pitch and professional bios takes time and iteration. Experiment with different versions, seek feedback and continuously refine them to effectively represent your personal brand and leave a lasting impression. A well-crafted elevator pitch and professional bios can open doors to opportunities, make networking interactions more impactful, and strengthen your overall personal brand.

### Example

Imagine you are attending a networking event and someone asks you to introduce yourself. Deliver a concise and impactful elevator pitch that summarizes your professional background, key skills, and unique value proposition. Additionally, ensure your professional bios on social media platforms, such as LinkedIn, effectively showcase your achievements, experiences, and areas of expertise.

## Mastering Public Speaking and Presentations

Mastering public speaking and presentations is a valuable skill that can greatly enhance your personal brand and boost your professional credibility. In this section, we explore strategies to help you deliver impactful and engaging speeches and presentations:

- Prepare and Rehearse: Thoroughly prepare your content, structure your speech or presentation, and rehearse it multiple times. Familiarize yourself with the key points, transitions, and supporting materials to ensure a smooth delivery.

- Connect with Your Audience: Establish a connection with your audience by understanding their needs, interests, and expectations. Tailor your message to resonate with them and use relatable examples or stories to capture their attention.

- Engage through Visuals and Multimedia: Utilize visuals, slides, or multimedia elements to enhance your presentation. Use compelling graphics, images, or videos that support your key points and help convey your message effectively.

- Use Body Language and Vocal Variety: Pay attention to your body language, facial expressions, and voice modulation. Maintain good posture, make eye contact with the audience, and vary your tone, pace, and volume to keep the audience engaged.

- Practice Active Listening: Incorporate opportunities for audience engagement and interaction during your presentation. Encourage questions, facilitate discussions, and actively listen to your audience's feedback or concerns.

- Handle Nervousness and Manage Stage Fright: Acknowledge and manage any nervousness or stage fright by practicing deep breathing, visualizing success, and reframing negative thoughts. Embrace the excitement of sharing your knowledge and passion with others.

- Seek Feedback and Continuously Improve: Solicit feedback from trusted peers, mentors, or speaking groups to identify areas for improvement. Actively incorporate the feedback into your future speaking engagements to refine your skills.

Mastering public speaking and presentations takes practice and experience. Embrace opportunities to speak in front of others, such as joining Toastmasters or participating in public speaking events. By honing your speaking skills, you can effectively convey your personal brand, inspire and influence others, and leave a lasting impact in professional settings.

Self-activity

Engage in a self-activity where you prepare a short presentation on a topic of your choice. Pay attention to structuring your content, using visual aids to enhance understanding, and incorporating storytelling techniques to engage your audience. Practice your delivery multiple times, focusing on confident and clear communication. Seek feedback to refine your presentation skills.

## Utilizing Storytelling to Convey Your Personal Brand

Storytelling is a powerful tool that can help you effectively communicate your personal brand and leave a lasting impact on your audience. In this section, we explore how you can leverage storytelling techniques to convey your personal brand:

- Identify Key Messages: Determine the key messages and values you want to convey through your stories. What aspects of your personal brand do you want to highlight? Craft stories that align with these messages and demonstrate your unique qualities and experiences.

- Use Personal Anecdotes: Incorporate personal anecdotes and experiences that showcase your journey, challenges, and successes. These stories create a human connection and make your personal brand relatable and memorable to your audience.

- Engage Emotions: Effective storytelling taps into emotions. Share stories that evoke empathy, inspire, or provoke thought. Connect with your audience on an emotional level to make a deeper impact and create a lasting impression.

- Keep it Relevant: Ensure that your stories are relevant to your personal brand and the context in which you are sharing them. Tailor your stories to the specific audience and the purpose of your communication.

- Structure your Stories: Craft your stories with a clear beginning, middle, and end. Build suspense, provide details, and deliver a satisfying conclusion. Use storytelling techniques such as vivid descriptions, dialogues, and imagery to make your stories engaging.

- Practice Authenticity: Be genuine and authentic in your storytelling. Share stories that reflect your true self and values. Authenticity resonates with audiences and helps build trust and credibility for your personal brand.

- Adapt for Different Platforms: Tailor your storytelling approach to different platforms, whether it's a presentation, social media post, or networking event. Adjust the length, tone, and level of detail to suit the platform and audience.

By utilizing storytelling to convey your personal brand, you can captivate your audience, create a memorable impression, and differentiate yourself from others. Craft compelling stories that highlight your unique qualities, experiences, and values, and watch as your personal brand becomes more impactful and influential.

## Conclusion

This chapter provided valuable insights and practical activities to develop effective communication skills. By enhancing verbal and written communication, crafting persuasive elevator pitches and professional bios, mastering public speaking and presentations, and utilizing storytelling, you can convey your personal brand with confidence and impact. In the next chapter, we will explore strategies for leveraging digital platforms and social media to enhance your personal brand presence.

# Chapter 7 | Showcasing Your Expertise

Here, we will focus on the importance of showcasing your expertise to establish yourself as a thought leader in your field. By creating valuable content, participating in industry events and conferences, and leveraging professional associations and online communities, you can effectively demonstrate your knowledge and build a strong professional reputation. This chapter provides strategies for positioning yourself as a thought leader, creating impactful content, maximizing your presence at industry events, and utilizing the power of professional associations and online communities.

## Establishing Yourself as a Thought Leader

Becoming a thought leader positions you as an authority in your field and increases your visibility and credibility. This section explores techniques for establishing yourself as a thought leader.

- Identifying your niche and areas of expertise: For example, if you are in the marketing field, you can establish yourself as a thought leader in digital marketing or content marketing.

- Consistently sharing valuable insights and perspectives: Write blog posts, publish articles, or create videos that offer valuable tips, industry trends, and thought-provoking analysis.

- Building a strong personal brand through consistent messaging: Develop a clear and compelling personal brand that aligns with your expertise and consistently communicates it through various channels.

- Engaging in conversations and thought-provoking discussions: Participate in industry forums, social media groups, and online communities to share your insights and engage in meaningful discussions with peers.

- Collaborating with other industry experts: Collaborate on projects, co-author articles or whitepapers, or contribute to joint webinars or podcasts to leverage the expertise of others and expand your reach.

## Example

John, a seasoned engineer, established himself as a thought leader in sustainable energy by consistently sharing his expertise through articles published in industry magazines and his personal blog. He engaged in discussions on online forums and social media platforms, offering valuable insights on renewable energy technologies and advocating for environmentally friendly practices. John also collaborated with researchers and academics to co-author research papers and present at industry conferences, further solidifying his reputation as a thought leader in the field.

## Creating Valuable Content

Creating valuable content is an effective way to showcase your expertise and provide value to your target audience. This section explores strategies for creating impactful content.

- Identifying the needs and interests of your target audience: Conduct market research and engage with your audience to understand their challenges and interests.

- Choosing the right content format, such as articles, videos, or podcasts: Tailor your content format to best resonate with your target audience.

- Developing a content creation and distribution plan: Consistently produce high-quality content and leverage various channels, such as your website, social media platforms, or industry publications, to distribute it.

- Consistently producing high-quality and relevant content: Provide valuable insights, actionable advice, and in-depth analysis that addresses the pain points of your audience.

- Engaging with your audience and encouraging interaction: Respond to comments, questions, and feedback from your audience to foster meaningful connections and establish yourself as a reliable resource.

Example

Sarah, a finance expert, created a series of informative videos on her YouTube channel, addressing common financial misconceptions and providing practical tips for personal financial management. She also authored a blog where she regularly published articles on investment strategies, retirement planning, and tax optimization. By consistently creating valuable content, Sarah attracted a large following and established herself as a trusted authority in personal finance.

## Participating in Industry Events and Conferences

Industry events and conferences provide opportunities to network, learn from experts, and showcase your expertise to a wider audience. This section provides strategies for maximizing your presence at industry events.

- Researching and selecting relevant events and conferences: Identify conferences, trade shows, and seminars that align with your industry and target audience.

- Preparing and delivering impactful presentations or speeches: Develop engaging presentations that highlight your expertise and offer valuable insights to the audience.

- Actively participating in panel discussions and Q&A sessions: Engage in interactive sessions to share your knowledge, answer questions, and showcase your expertise.

- Networking with fellow professionals and industry influencers: Connect with peers, potential clients, and industry leaders during networking sessions and social events.

- Following up with contacts and nurturing relationships post-event: Maintain contact with individuals you meet at events to foster long-term professional relationships.

List of popular industry events & conferences
**Engineering & Technology"**

- International Conference on Engineering and Technology (ICET)
- World Congress on Engineering (WCE)
- IEEE International Conference on Robotics and Automation (ICRA)
- Society of Automotive Engineers (SAE) International Conference
- Consumer Electronics Show (CES)

- Web Summit
- Google I/O
- Microsoft Ignite

## Business and Finance:

- World Economic Forum (WEF) Annual Meeting
- Forbes Under 30 Summit
- TED Conference
- Harvard Business Review Summit
- Financial Times Global Banking Summit
- Bloomberg New Economy Forum

## Operations & Supply Chain:

- Council of Supply Chain Management Professionals (CSCMP) Annual Conference
- Institute for Supply Management (ISM) Annual Conference
- Manufacturing Leadership Summit
- Operations Summit
- International Association of Six Sigma Certification (IASSC) Conference

## Medical Devices:

- Medical Design & Manufacturing (MD&M) West
- The MedTech Conference
- Medical Device Innovation Summit
- BIOMEDevice Conference

**Healthcare:**

- Healthcare Information and Management Systems Society (HIMSS) Conference
- World Health Summit
- World Healthcare Congress
- Mayo Clinic Transform Conference
- Health 2.0 Conference

## Leveraging Professional Associations and Online Communities

Professional associations and online communities offer platforms for networking, knowledge-sharing, and establishing your professional presence. This section explores strategies for leveraging these platforms effectively.

- Researching and joining relevant professional associations and organizations: Identify associations and organizations that cater to your industry or area of expertise.

- Actively participating in discussions and sharing insights: Engage in online forums, LinkedIn groups, or industry-specific communities to contribute to conversations and share your expertise.

- Contributing to forums, blogs, or social media groups: Provide valuable insights and offer practical solutions to industry challenges in relevant online platforms.

- Seeking leadership opportunities within associations or communities: Volunteer for leadership roles, committee memberships, or speaking opportunities within professional associations to enhance your visibility and demonstrate your commitment to the field.

- Building meaningful connections with industry peers: Connect with fellow professionals in your industry through networking events, online platforms, and industry-specific meetups.

Example

Michael, a software engineer, joined a professional association for software development and actively participated in their online forums. He shared his insights on emerging technologies, best coding practices, and problem-solving techniques, providing valuable contributions to discussions. Michael also volunteered as a mentor for junior developers, offering guidance and support. Through his active involvement in the association, he built strong connections with fellow professionals, expanding his network and establishing himself as a respected member of the software development community.


## Conclusion

Chapter 7 has explored strategies for showcasing your expertise by establishing yourself as a thought leader, creating valuable content, participating in industry events and conferences, and leveraging professional associations and online communities. By implementing these strategies, you can effectively showcase your knowledge, expand your professional network, and strengthen your reputation as an expert in your field. In the next chapter, we will delve into the importance of continuous learning and professional development for long-term career growth.

# Chapter 8 | Building a Reputation for Excellence

This chapter explores the importance of building a reputation for excellence in your professional journey. By going above and beyond in your work, developing a strong work ethic, continuously learning and growing, and managing your personal brand within your organization, you can establish yourself as a valuable asset and cultivate a reputation for excellence. This chapter provides insights and strategies to help you excel in your career and gain recognition within your organization.

## Going Above and Beyond in Your Work

To build a reputation for excellence, it is essential to consistently deliver high-quality work and exceed expectations. This section explores strategies for going above and beyond in your work by setting ambitious goals, demonstrating initiative and proactivity, seeking additional responsibilities, delivering exceptional quality, and providing innovative solutions.

- Setting ambitious goals is a powerful motivator that pushes you to achieve exceptional results. By challenging yourself with ambitious targets, you push the boundaries of what you thought possible and strive for excellence.

- Demonstrating initiative and proactivity is another key aspect of going above and beyond. Instead of waiting for instructions, take the initiative to identify new opportunities or challenges within your role. By being proactive, you showcase your willingness to contribute and make a positive impact.

- Seeking additional responsibilities is an effective way to go above and beyond in your work. Volunteer for projects or tasks that stretch your skills and showcase your abilities. This not only demonstrates your commitment to your organization but also provides valuable opportunities for growth and development.

- Delivering exceptional quality is essential for building a reputation for excellence. Paying attention to detail, ensuring accuracy, and consistently producing high-quality work showcase your dedication to excellence and professionalism.

- Providing innovative solutions is another way to go above and beyond. Think creatively and offer innovative ideas and solutions to problems or challenges. This demonstrates your ability to think outside the box and add value to your organization.

By implementing these strategies and consistently going above and beyond in your work, you will not only stand out from your peers but also gain the respect and recognition of your colleagues and superiors.

## Developing a Strong Work Ethic

A strong work ethic is crucial for building a reputation for excellence. This section explores strategies for developing and maintaining a strong work ethic.

Demonstrating reliability and punctuality is essential in establishing a strong work ethic. Consistently meeting deadlines, fulfilling commitments, and being punctual for meetings and assignments shows your colleagues and superiors that they can rely on you to deliver results.

Taking ownership of your work is another important aspect of a strong work ethic. By taking responsibility for your projects, tasks, and outcomes, you demonstrate accountability and a commitment to excellence. This includes acknowledging mistakes, learning from them, and taking corrective actions when necessary.

Embracing a positive attitude is crucial in maintaining a strong work ethic. Approaching challenges with optimism and perseverance enables you to navigate obstacles and setbacks more effectively. A positive attitude not only enhances your own productivity but also influences those around you, creating a positive work environment.

Practicing discipline and time management is key to maintaining a strong work ethic. Prioritizing tasks, managing your time effectively, and avoiding procrastination enable you to stay focused and accomplish your work efficiently. This includes setting realistic goals, creating schedules, and utilizing productivity techniques to maximize your productivity.

Emphasizing integrity and ethical conduct is an integral part of a strong work ethic. Upholding ethical standards, demonstrating honesty, and maintaining confidentiality build trust and credibility. Acting with integrity in all aspects of your work reinforces your reputation for excellence.

By developing and consistently practicing a strong work ethic, you not only showcase your professionalism and commitment to excellence but also create a positive impression on others, positioning yourself as a reliable and valuable asset within your organization.

## Continuous Learning and Professional Development

Continuous learning and professional development play a vital role in shaping a successful and fulfilling career. In a rapidly evolving professional landscape, staying stagnant can hinder your growth and limit your opportunities. By committing to lifelong learning and embracing professional development, you can enhance your knowledge, skills, and expertise, and position yourself as a valuable asset within your industry.

Pursuing relevant training and certifications is an effective way to stay ahead in your field. Identify areas for improvement and seek out training programs and certifications that align with your career goals. These programs provide you with specialized knowledge and skills that can make you more competitive and sought-after in your industry. Whether it's acquiring a project management certification or obtaining a data analytics specialization, these credentials demonstrate your commitment to professional growth and can open doors to new opportunities.

Actively seeking feedback and constructive criticism is crucial for personal and professional development. Request feedback from supervisors, peers, and mentors to gain insights into your strengths and areas for improvement. Embrace feedback as an opportunity for growth and make necessary changes to enhance your performance. Engaging in self-reflection and seeking continuous feedback allows you to continuously evolve and refine your skills.

Engaging in professional networking is a powerful way to expand your knowledge, gain exposure to new ideas, and build meaningful connections within your industry. Attend industry events, join professional associations, and actively participate in networking activities. Engaging with like-minded professionals provides opportunities to exchange insights, collaborate on projects, and stay updated on the latest trends and best practices. Building a strong professional network not only enhances your learning but also opens doors to new career opportunities.

Staying informed through industry publications is essential for professional development. Regularly reading industry-specific publications, books, and articles keeps you abreast of the latest developments, emerging trends, and thought leadership in your field. Subscribe to relevant newsletters, follow influential professionals on social media, and engage in online discussions to stay connected with the pulse of your industry.

Embracing new challenges and opportunities is a mindset that fosters continuous growth. Seek out projects or responsibilities that push you out of your comfort zone and allow for personal and professional development. Embracing new challenges not only expands your skill set but also demonstrates your adaptability and willingness to take on new roles and responsibilities.

List of Popular Continuous Learning and Professional Development Programs:
- Coursera: Offers a wide range of online courses and certifications from top universities and institutions.

- LinkedIn Learning: Provides a vast library of online courses covering various professional skills and development areas.
- Udemy: Offers a diverse selection of online courses taught by industry experts across different fields.
- Harvard Business School Online: Provides online business courses and programs designed to enhance leadership and management skills.
- edX: Offers online courses from top universities and institutions worldwide, covering a wide range of subjects.
- Skillshare: Provides a platform for creative professionals to access online classes and workshops in areas such as design, photography, and writing.
- Project Management Institute (PMI): Offers certifications and professional development opportunities for project management professionals.
- Society for Human Resource Management (SHRM): Provides resources, certifications, and professional development opportunities for HR professionals.
- Toastmasters International: Offers public speaking and leadership development programs to improve communication and presentation skills.
- International Institute of Business Analysis (IIBA): Provides certifications and resources for business analysts to enhance their skills and knowledge.

By actively engaging in continuous learning and professional development, you demonstrate your commitment to excellence and career advancement. The pursuit of knowledge, skills, and experiences positions you as a proactive and forward-thinking professional within your industry. By embracing these strategies and participating in popular continuous learning and professional development programs, you can stay relevant, expand your expertise, and enhance your reputation for excellence in your respective field.

# Chapter 9 | Navigating Challenges and Overcoming Obstacles

In this last chapter of this book, we explore the dynamic landscape of personal branding, acknowledging that it is not without its fair share of challenges and obstacles. Building a strong personal brand requires perseverance, adaptability, and a positive mindset. This chapter equips you with valuable strategies to effectively navigate common challenges, handle criticism and negative feedback, cultivate resilience, and harness the power of failures as stepping stones to growth.

## Common Challenges in Personal Branding

Building a personal brand is a multi-faceted endeavor that presents its own set of challenges. In this section, we delve deeper into the common obstacles professionals often encounter on their personal branding journey. By understanding and addressing these challenges, you can navigate your path more effectively and enhance your personal brand with greater confidence.

Establishing credibility is vital for personal branding as it allows you to gain trust, credibility, and recognition in your industry or field of expertise. When you are seen as a credible professional, others are more likely to listen to your insights, value your opinions, and consider you a reliable source of information. Here are some strategies to help you establish and enhance your credibility:

- Thought Leadership Content: Share your expertise and insights through thought leadership content. This can include writing articles, blog posts, or whitepapers that demonstrate your knowledge and provide valuable information to your target audience. By consistently delivering high-quality content, you position yourself as an authority in your field and build credibility.

- Showcase Achievements and Credentials: Highlight your relevant achievements, credentials, and qualifications. This can include academic degrees, certifications, awards, and professional accomplishments. Displaying these accomplishments on your website, social media profiles, or professional bio helps establish your expertise and credibility.

- Engage in Industry Discussions and Forums: Actively participate in industry discussions, forums, and social media groups related to your field. Share your insights, provide helpful answers to questions, and engage with others in a meaningful way. By contributing valuable information and being a helpful resource, you build credibility and gain visibility within your industry.

- Seek Testimonials and Recommendations: Request testimonials and recommendations from clients, colleagues, or industry leaders who have worked with you or experienced the value you provide. Testimonials serve as social proof and can significantly enhance your credibility. Display these testimonials on your website or include them in your marketing materials.

- Collaborate with Influencers and Experts: Collaborating with influencers or industry experts can boost your credibility by association. Seek opportunities to collaborate on projects, co-author content, or participate in panel discussions or podcasts with established professionals in your field. This can help you leverage their credibility and expand your own reach.

- Maintain Professionalism and Integrity: Consistently demonstrating professionalism, integrity, and ethical behavior is essential for building and maintaining credibility. Be reliable, deliver on your promises, and conduct yourself with authenticity and transparency. Building a reputation for professionalism and trustworthiness will enhance your personal brand's credibility.

Self-doubt is another common challenge and significant hurdle that can hinder personal branding progress. It can manifest as imposter syndrome, fear of failure, or the belief that others are more qualified or talented. It is that nagging voice in your head that questions your abilities, compares you to others, and undermines your confidence. Overcoming self-doubt is crucial for building a strong personal brand and embracing your unique value. Here are some strategies to help you navigate and conquer self-doubt:

- Cultivate Self-Awareness: Start by becoming aware of your thoughts and emotions when self-doubt arises. Recognize the patterns and triggers that fuel self-doubt. By acknowledging and understanding these patterns, you can take proactive steps to address them.

- Focus on Your Strengths: Shift your focus from your perceived weaknesses to your strengths. Identify your unique skills, experiences, and qualities that make you stand out. Celebrate your achievements and remind yourself of past successes. Developing a positive self-image based on your strengths will help counteract self-doubt.

- Embrace Growth Mindset: Adopt a growth mindset, which is the belief that abilities and talents can be developed through dedication and hard work. Understand that personal growth is a continuous journey, and setbacks are opportunities for learning and improvement. Embracing a growth mindset allows you to view challenges as stepping stones toward success.

- Seek Support and Validation: Surround yourself with a supportive network of mentors, peers, and friends who believe in your abilities. Seek their guidance and feedback. Having a support system can provide reassurance and help you gain perspective when self-doubt arises.

- Reframe Negative Thoughts: Challenge negative self-talk and replace it with positive and empowering thoughts. When self-doubt creeps in, consciously reframe those thoughts by focusing on your accomplishments, reminding yourself of your capabilities, and visualizing your desired outcomes. Practice affirmations to reinforce positive beliefs about yourself.

- Take Action and Embrace Failure: One of the most effective ways to overcome self-doubt is to take action. Start small and gradually push yourself out of your comfort zone. Embrace failures as learning opportunities and understand that setbacks are a natural part of growth. Use failures as motivation to improve and move forward.

Remember that self-doubt is a common experience, and even the most successful individuals have faced it at some point. The key is not to let self-doubt paralyze you or hold you back from pursuing your goals. By cultivating self-awareness, focusing on your strengths, adopting a growth mindset, seeking support, reframing negative thoughts, and taking action, you can overcome self-doubt and build a resilient personal brand that reflects your true potential.

## Dealing with Criticism and Negative Feedback

Criticism and negative feedback are inevitable in any professional journey, including personal branding. Learning how to handle criticism effectively and constructively can contribute to your personal growth and resilience. In this section, we explore strategies to help you constructively navigate criticism and negative feedback:

- Embrace a Growth Mindset: Adopting a growth mindset is essential when faced with criticism. Instead of viewing criticism as a personal attack or a reflection of your worth, see it as an opportunity for growth and improvement. Understand that feedback can provide valuable insights and help you identify areas for development.

- Separate Valid Feedback from Trolls: Not all feedback is constructive or valuable. Learn to discern between genuine, well-intentioned feedback and unproductive criticism or trolling. Consider the source of the feedback, their expertise, and the specific points they raise. Focus on feedback that can genuinely help you refine your personal brand and ignore baseless negativity.

- Seek Constructive Feedback: Actively seek out constructive feedback from trusted mentors, peers, or industry professionals who can provide valuable insights. Request specific feedback on areas you are looking to improve and ask for actionable suggestions for growth. By seeking constructive feedback proactively, you can gain valuable perspectives and refine your personal brand.

- Respond Positively and Professionally: When faced with criticism or negative feedback, respond with professionalism and positivity. Avoid reacting defensively or engaging in heated arguments. Instead, take a step back, analyze the feedback objectively, and respond in a composed manner. Acknowledge the feedback, express gratitude for the insights, and share your commitment to continuous improvement.

- Learn from Criticism: Look for opportunities to learn and grow from criticism. Consider the underlying message behind the feedback and evaluate if there are areas where you can genuinely improve. Use criticism as a catalyst for self-reflection and professional development. Embrace the mindset of constant improvement and view feedback as a valuable tool for honing your personal brand.

- Surround Yourself with Support: Build a network of supportive individuals who can provide encouragement and guidance during challenging times. Seek support from mentors, peers, or friends who believe in your abilities and can offer a fresh perspective. Having a support system can help you navigate criticism more effectively and maintain a positive mindset.

- Focus on the Positive: While it's essential to address and learn from criticism, it's equally important to focus on the positive aspects of your personal brand. Celebrate your achievements, recognize your strengths, and remind yourself of the value you bring. By maintaining a positive mindset and focusing on your growth and progress, you can build resilience and overcome the impact of negative feedback.

Remember, criticism is not a reflection of your worth as a professional. It is an opportunity for growth and improvement. By embracing a growth mindset, seeking constructive feedback, responding positively and professionally, learning from criticism, surrounding yourself with support, and focusing on the positive aspects of your personal brand, you can navigate criticism and negative feedback with resilience and continue to enhance your personal brand.

## Building Resilience and Maintaining a Positive Mindset

Resilience is crucial in overcoming challenges and maintaining momentum in your personal branding journey. In the face of challenges and setbacks, resilience helps you bounce back, adapt, and continue pursuing your goals. A positive mindset enables you to maintain motivation, overcome obstacles, and embrace growth opportunities. In this section, we explore strategies to build resilience and cultivate a positive mindset:

Embrace a Growth Mindset: Adopting a growth mindset is foundational to building resilience and maintaining a positive mindset. Embrace the belief that challenges and setbacks are opportunities for learning and growth. Instead of viewing failures as permanent, see them as temporary setbacks that can be overcome with effort and perseverance.

A growth mindset empowers you to approach challenges with resilience and optimism.

- Cultivate Self-Compassion: Treat yourself with kindness and compassion during difficult times. Acknowledge that everyone faces challenges and setbacks along their journey. Practice self-care, engage in activities that bring you joy and relaxation, and be mindful of your physical and emotional well-being. By nurturing self-compassion, you build resilience and maintain a positive outlook.

- Develop Coping Strategies: Identify and develop coping strategies that work for you in times of stress or adversity. This could include engaging in mindfulness practices, practicing deep breathing exercises, journaling, or seeking support from a trusted friend or mentor. Find healthy outlets to express and process your emotions, which can help you stay balanced and focused on your personal brand goals.

- Focus on Solutions, Not Problems: When faced with challenges, shift your focus from dwelling on the problem to seeking solutions. Break down complex issues into smaller, manageable tasks and take proactive steps to address them. By focusing on solutions, you maintain a positive mindset and build confidence in your ability to overcome obstacles.

- Celebrate Progress and Successes: Recognize and celebrate even the smallest wins along your personal branding journey. Acknowledge your progress, accomplishments, and milestones. By celebrating your successes, you reinforce a positive mindset and fuel your motivation to keep moving forward.

- Surround Yourself with Positive Influences: Surround yourself with individuals who uplift and inspire you. Seek positive role models, mentors, or peers who support your personal branding goals and share a similar mindset. Engage in meaningful conversations, participate in supportive communities, and learn from those who radiate positivity and resilience.

## Learning from Failures and Growing

Failures are an integral part of personal and professional growth. However, it's how we respond to and learn from these failures that can make all the difference. In this section, we explore the importance of embracing failures as learning opportunities and growing from them:

- Shift Your Perspective: Instead of viewing failures as setbacks or indicators of incompetence, reframe them as valuable learning experiences. Embrace the mindset that failure is a stepping stone to success and an opportunity for growth. By shifting your perspective, you can extract valuable lessons from your failures and use them to improve your personal brand.

- Analyze the Root Causes: When faced with failure, take the time to analyze the root causes and factors that contributed to it. Identify any mistakes, gaps in knowledge or skills, or areas for improvement. This introspection will help you pinpoint specific areas where you can grow and develop.

- Learn from Mistakes: Mistakes often serve as powerful teachers. Reflect on the mistakes you've made and consider the lessons they offer. What could you have done differently? What skills or knowledge could you have applied? Use this information to enhance your personal brand and refine your strategies moving forward.

- Adapt and Pivot: Failures provide opportunities to adapt and pivot your approach. Use the insights gained from your failures to make necessary adjustments to your personal branding strategies.

This might involve refining your messaging, targeting a different audience, or exploring new avenues for growth. Flexibility and adaptability are key to turning failures into stepping stones toward success.

- Seek Feedback and Support: Don't hesitate to seek feedback and support from mentors, peers, or trusted professionals. They can provide valuable insights and perspectives on your failures, helping you gain new perspectives and identify blind spots. Their guidance and support can assist you in learning from your failures and growing as a result.

- Persevere and Stay Resilient: It's important to remain resilient and maintain a sense of determination in the face of failures. Understand that setbacks are a natural part of the journey and that success often requires perseverance. Use failures as fuel to propel you forward, learning from each setback and continuing to grow in pursuit of your personal branding goals.

- Embrace Continuous Learning: Personal branding is an ongoing process, and failures offer valuable opportunities for continuous learning. Embrace a mindset of lifelong learning and commit to continuously improving yourself and your personal brand. Seek out learning experiences, attend workshops or courses, and stay updated with industry trends to enhance your knowledge and skills.

## Conclusion

In this chapter, we explored the common challenges in personal branding and provided strategies to overcome them. We delved into dealing with criticism and negative feedback, building resilience and maintaining a positive mindset, learning from failures, and growing. The key takeaway from this chapter is that challenges and obstacles are inevitable in the journey of personal branding, but they can be transformed into opportunities for growth and development.

By embracing a growth mindset, individuals can reframe challenges as learning experiences and use them to refine their personal brand. It is crucial to handle criticism and negative feedback constructively, seeking valuable insights and filtering out unproductive negativity. Building resilience and maintaining a positive mindset enable individuals to bounce back from setbacks, stay motivated, and navigate the ups and downs of their personal branding journey.

Learning from failures is an essential part of personal growth. Embracing failures as stepping stones toward success allows individuals to analyze their mistakes, adapt their strategies, and persevere in the pursuit of their personal branding goals. By cultivating a mindset of continuous learning and seeking feedback and support, individuals can continuously refine their personal brand and stay ahead in their chosen fields.

Overall, the key message is that challenges and obstacles should not deter individuals from their personal branding journey. Instead, they should be seen as opportunities for growth, learning, and self-improvement. By navigating challenges with resilience, maintaining a positive mindset, learning from failures, and growing through the process, individuals can build a strong and authentic personal brand that sets them apart and propels them toward professional success.

# Summary

Congratulations on reaching the summary of "The Power of Personal Branding: Stand Out and Thrive in Your Career"! Throughout this book, we have explored the various aspects of personal branding and how it can empower you to achieve exceptional career growth. As we conclude this journey, let's recap the key takeaways, provide actionable steps for strengthening your personal brand, and reflect on the importance of personal branding for career success.

## Recap of Key Takeaways

1. Your personal brand is the unique combination of your skills, experiences, values, and reputation that sets you apart from others.

2. Personal branding requires self-awareness, defining your brand attributes, and aligning them with your career goals.

3. Authenticity and consistency are crucial in building a strong personal brand that resonates with your target audience.

4. Soft skills, such as effective communication, networking, and leadership, play a vital role in enhancing your personal brand.

5. Building and nurturing professional relationships, including mentors and sponsors, can accelerate your career growth.

6. Continuous learning, adaptability, and a positive mindset are key to overcoming challenges and growing from failures.

7. Showcasing your expertise through thought leadership, valuable content, and participation in industry events can elevate your personal brand.

8. Building a reputation for excellence requires going above and beyond in your work, developing a strong work ethic, and managing your personal brand within your organization.


## Actionable Steps for Strengthening Your Personal Brand

1. Define your personal brand attributes and values.

2. Conduct a self-audit to identify areas for improvement and skill development.

3. Craft a compelling elevator pitch and professional bios that effectively communicate your unique value proposition.

4. Enhance your verbal and written communication skills through practice and feedback.

5. Embrace storytelling as a powerful tool to convey your personal brand.

6. Build a strong network by actively participating in networking events and leveraging online platforms.

7. Seek out mentors and sponsors who can guide and support your career growth.

8. Develop a continuous learning plan and invest in professional development programs, workshops, and courses.

9. Create valuable content that showcases your expertise and engages your target audience.

10. Actively participate in industry events and conferences to expand your network and gain visibility.

*Summary*

# Final Thoughts

## Importance of Personal Branding for Career Success

Personal branding is not just a buzzword; it is a fundamental element for career success in today's competitive landscape. Your personal brand serves as your unique value proposition, differentiating you from others and positioning you as an authority in your field. It opens doors to new opportunities, expands your network, and allows you to leave a lasting impression on others.

Investing in your personal brand is an investment in your professional future. By consciously shaping and nurturing your personal brand, you have the power to shape your career trajectory and create meaningful opportunities. It enables you to stand out, gain recognition, and unlock doors that may have otherwise remained closed.

Remember, personal branding is a continuous journey. It requires ongoing effort, self-reflection, and adaptation to stay relevant and impactful. Embrace the process, remain authentic, and let your unique story and expertise shine.

## Final Thoughts

*Thank you for joining us on this transformative journey. May your personal brand continue to evolve and propel you toward extraordinary career growth and fulfillment. Best of luck in all your endeavors!*